Read What These Christian Leaders Are Saying About Kate McVeigh

"I highly recommend Kate McVeigh's ministry and her new book, *The Favor Factor*. Get ready to triumph over temptations, tests, and trials by the force of favor that is found in this new book."

Ronnie Sims
Pastor, Word of Life Church
Jackson, Mississippi

"This book brings to light a clear understanding on how favor can work for you. I highly recommend reading this book. It will bless you!"

Mac Gober
Canaan Land Ministries
Autaugaville, Alabama

"Kate McVeigh believes God and will not quit. This spirit of faith is evident in her book, *The Favor Factor*."

Scott Webb
Pastor, Word of Life Christian Center
Birmingham, Alabama

"Kate McVeigh is a bright young woman diligently fulfilling God's purpose and call on her life by reaching as many people as possible for the Lord Jesus Christ. We support Kate's radio ministry with our prayers and finances on a monthly basis because we have seen her heart and believe in what she is doing."

Dave and Joyce Meyer
Joyce Meyer Ministries
Fenton, Missouri

"Rev. Kate McVeigh is a faithful member of RHEMA Bible Church, attending services and participating as her itinerant ministry schedule permits. I know Kate to be a dedicated and talented minister of the Gospel. She has a desire to reach the lost for Jesus Christ and to help encourage believers in their daily Christian walk.

"As Kate's pastor, I am proud of her ministerial accomplishments and am excited about her new book, *The Favor Factor.*"

Kenneth Hagin Jr.
Pastor/Executive Vice-President
RHEMA Bible Church
RHEMA Bible Training Center
Kenneth Hagin Ministries

The Favor Factor

**Releasing God's
Supernatural Influence
To Work for You**

The Favor Factor

Releasing God's
Supernatural Influence
To Work for You

by
Kate McVeigh

Harrison House
Tulsa, Oklahoma

3rd Printing

The Favor Factor — Releasing God's Supernatural Influence To Work for You
ISBN 0-89274-967-9
Copyright © 1997 by Kate McVeigh
P. O. Box 690753
Tulsa, Oklahoma 74169-0753

Published by Harrison House, Inc.
P. O. Box 35035
Tulsa, Oklahoma 74153

Contents

Acknowledgments

It is with great appreciation that I wish to thank some very special people for their help with this book:

Donna Larson for your input and research.

Pastor Clarence King for teaching me about the favor of God.

And a very special thank you to Karen Jensen without whom this book would never have made the deadline: Thanks for helping me put in writing what was in my heart.

1
God's Favor Changed Me!

1
God's Favor Changed Me!

When I was a teenager in high school, I felt as though no one liked me. I had been in Special Education classes for slow learners from the time I was in the fifth grade. All the other kids made fun of me. I developed an overwhelming inferiority complex.

Everywhere I went I felt that no one cared about me. I felt they thought that I was dumb and, because I wore braces, I was ugly. One time I even asked my sister Helen if I was retarded. I thought something was really wrong with me and that my family and friends wouldn't tell me because they didn't want to hurt my feelings.

Everywhere I went I expected people to reject me. And guess what? They did! For example, out of my school class of more than 600 kids, I was nominated "Least Likely To Succeed"!

I loved to play basketball, but all the girls on the team were really mean to me. They used to tell me I was stupid and retarded. They nicknamed me "Sped" because I was in Special Ed. I felt so terrible about myself that I often wanted to commit suicide.

Transformed by God's Power

When I turned sixteen, though, something happened to me. My mother received the Lord and was healed of several physical conditions. She began to share the goodness and love of God with me.

Several weeks later a man by the name of Kenneth E. Hagin came to hold a crusade in my hometown of Detroit, Michigan. My mother invited me to go with her to the crusade. I did, along with my aunt and cousins.

I went the first night. When Brother Hagin gave the altar call, something inside me really wanted to go forward because I knew I needed to be saved. But I was too embarrassed because my cousins were there — it was all so new to me. I went to church only on Christmas and Easter, and I had never even opened a Bible.

After the altar call, Brother Hagin prayed, "Lord, if there is anyone here who doesn't know You as Savior, I pray that they won't be able to eat or sleep or find any rest until they make You the Lord of their life."

When I went home I couldn't sleep all night, thinking about what he had prayed. The next night I just knew I had to go back.

I waited through the whole service, and this time when the altar call came, I went forward with all the others. My heart was pounding. As I stood there, I lifted one hand toward heaven and gave my heart to Jesus. Then, as hands were laid upon me, I was filled with the Holy Ghost. My life was changed!

Favor Heals Insecurities

Shortly after that, as I began to study God's Word, I started to realize how His love and favor could heal the insecurities in my life. I learned that, because I had become His very own dearly beloved child, my heavenly Father had poured His love, abundant blessing and divine favor upon me!

One of the first things I did after receiving Jesus was to find a good Bible-believing church. I'm so glad that my pastor was teaching on the subject of God's favor! He continually taught that we can claim favor in every area of life and related how he walked in favor in his own life.

Our congregation learned that if there were going to be a raise given on the job, we could get it because of God's favor. If there were a good deal to be found, we would find it. If there were an impossible situation facing us, God would change it. We found out we could have favor with our teachers, families, friends, bosses and other business contacts.

Finally, I started confessing that I had favor with all my teachers, friends and family. Even now, I don't start the day without saying, "Lord, I thank You that I have favor with You and man this day. People go out of their way to bless me and to do good to me today." I meditated on Psalm 5:12 (NKJV):

> **For You, O Lord, will bless the righteous; with favor You will surround him as with a shield.**

I also began to claim favor with my basketball team. Our coach hardly ever let me play in games because I was so timid and always made mistakes.

I was a good basketball player, really, but no one on the team had seen that side of me. I could play great at home with my brothers, but when I got around the girls at school, I grew so insecure that my hands would shake. When it came time to shoot the ball, I would freeze because I was so nervous.

Once I heard my pastor's teaching on favor, I stopped looking at the old Kate — the one who always was rejected by the team. Instead, I began to see myself walking in God's favor. I had to choose to see myself the way God sees me.

I started saying I had favor with my coach and with all my teammates — that I was no longer timid but confident — because God's favor was working on my behalf.

I prayed this way during my entire summer vacation. When I returned to school, I was a brand new person! My coach, friends and teachers were shocked to see the formerly shy, timid Kate transformed into one of the top basketball players on the high school team!

Until that time I couldn't even give an oral book report without thinking I would pass out. Now I was preaching the Gospel! Other students looked to me as a spiritual leader, and I was able to lead many other teenagers to Christ as they saw the dramatic changes in my life.

Let me encourage you as you read this book to begin to see who you really are in Christ — that in Him you are more than a conqueror (Romans 8:37), deeply loved (John 3:16, Ephesians 2:4), accepted by God (Ephesians 1:6) and made righteous through the blood of Jesus (2 Corinthians 5:21).

If you expect people to reject you and treat you improperly, they will. But when you *expect* God's favor to be demonstrated toward you, you will receive it in abundance!

2
What Is Divine Favor?

2

What Is Divine Favor?

**For You, O Lord, will bless the righteous; with
favor You will surround him as with a shield.**

Psalm 5:12 NKJV

If you are a born-again child of God, this Scripture is
talking about *you!*

The Bible tells us in Second Corinthians 5:21 that
because of Jesus' sacrifice we have been made **the
righteousness of God in him.** Through the blood of Jesus
we have been made right with God — the barrier and
separation that once existed because of sin have been done
away with, and we have obtained right standing with our
heavenly Father!

So, when the Bible declares that the Lord will bless "the
righteous" with favor, it means you and me!

In Webster's dictionary the definition of *favor* includes:
"friendly or kind regard; good will; approval; liking; unfair
partiality; favoritism"; "attractiveness"; "to be partial to;
prefer"; "to help; assist"; "to do a kindness for;"
"endorsing."[1]

To be *favored* means: "regarded or treated with favor";
"provided with advantages"; "specially privileged."[2]

Just think about that! God wants to give you special
privileges. The favor of God will cause people to go out of
their way to bless you without even knowing why they're
doing it. And the more you are blessed, the more you can be
a blessing.

19

Supernatural Favor

God's supernatural favor flowing in your life is not based on your background, looks or personality. His favor is based on the Word of God and believing what it says about you. Favor can break through any barriers set before you, and it is available to every child of God.

When you believe and activate your faith for God's favor, it will work for you. Someone may not particularly like you or your personality, but that doesn't matter. You're believing in God's ability to influence them, and His favor on your life is supernatural. In other words it supersedes natural circumstances.

Genesis 12:2 in *The Amplified Bible* says:

> **And I will make of you a great nation, and I will bless you [with abundant increase of favors] and make your name famous and distinguished, and you will be a blessing [dispensing good to others].**

This Scripture clearly shows that God wants to bless you with supernatural favor. He wants you to be blessed and to make you a blessing to everyone you meet.

We can see this kind of favor operating in the life of Daniel. He and all the Israelites were prisoners in Babylon. For reasons that can't be explained naturally, though, he had favor with the leaders of the land.

> **Now God had brought Daniel into favour and tender love with the prince of the eunuchs.**
>
> **Daniel 1:9**

In other accounts we learn that Daniel had so much favor with the leaders of the land, he was elevated to prestigious positions in the Babylonian kingdom.

Even though the circumstances were stacked against him, Daniel eventually became the prime minister of Babylon. Why did good things happen to Daniel? Because of God's favor. Daniel loved and trusted God and expected things to turn out well for him. As a matter of fact, Ephesians 6:24 says there is special favor for those who sincerely love Jesus:

Grace [favor] **be with all those who love our Lord Jesus Christ in sincerity** (NKJV).

You can be just like Daniel. Call yourself a success. Expect promotion to come your way. See yourself highly favored, with good things happening in your behalf. Confess it. Believe for the impossible! God's supernatural favor will work for you.

How To Activate Favor in Your Life

One way to reap a harvest of God's favor in your life is to *sow* favor. Make sure that you are helping someone else and showing favor to them. As it is said, "What you make happen for others, God will make happen for you."

Any time you plant a seed — whether it is in finances, friendship, favor or any other area — that seed leaves your hand but it doesn't leave your life. It is working in the supernatural realm, bringing you a harvest in that same area.

It's important to sow favor in order to reap it in your own life.

Endnotes

[1] *Webster's New World College Dictionary*, 3rd Ed., s.v. "favor."

[2] *Ibid.*, "favored."

3
Favor in Ministry

3
Favor in Ministry

In the book of Esther there is a story that wonderfully illustrates the favor of God.

Esther was a beautiful Jewish woman who became queen to King Ahasuerus, although the king was not aware that she was a Jew.

> **The king loved Esther more than all the other women, and she obtained grace and favor in his sight more than all the virgins; so he set the royal crown upon her head and made her queen instead of Vashti.**
> **Esther 2:17 NKJV**

Because of political circumstances in Persia, Esther had to take a stand for her people. Haman, a top advisor to King Ahasuerus, had devised a plan to destroy the entire Jewish nation in Persia, so Esther decided she must go before the king on behalf of her people.

In doing so, however, Esther was risking her life. Anyone entering the king's inner court without an invitation would be put to death — unless the king held out his golden scepter to them, signaling his favor.

> **So it was, when the king saw Queen Esther standing in the court, that she found favor in his sight, and the king held out to Esther the golden scepter that was in his hand.**
> **Esther 5:2 NKJV**

Time and again God granted Esther favor in the king's sight and the Jewish people were spared.

Just as God granted favor to Esther, so will He grant you favor in your life and ministry. Whether you are a pastor, teacher, evangelist, missionary or minister of helps, God wants to bless *you* with favor!

I started acting on the Word of God early in my Christian walk and began to confess Scriptures about the favor of God daily. When God called me to preach at age sixteen, He showed me His plan for my life — I would be teaching and preaching the Gospel throughout America and in other nations. But I wondered how could this come to pass — I didn't know even one pastor!

When God called me, He said that I didn't have to wait until I was thirty years old. I was to begin preaching the Gospel while I was young. Some people think that when you are young, single and a woman the odds are against you. But when you have the favor of God, that is not the case. Doors began to open supernaturally as His favor went to work on my behalf.

It is important to remember that promotion does not come from man but from God. (Psalm 75:6,7.) When the call of God is on your life, you never have to prove to anyone that you are anointed. Nor do you have to strive in the flesh to get doors to open. Doors of opportunity will open when we claim God's favor and allow Him to do the promoting.

In Colossians 4:3 Paul prayed that a door of utterance would be opened to him. Before I ever started preaching, I was believing and confessing God's favor daily. I would look at my empty calendar and say, "One day you will be too small to hold all the places that God will send me!"

I constantly confess that I have favor with pastors and their wives, and that God is adding financial partners to my ministry daily so that I can accomplish all He has called me to do. And I *have* favor!

Once when I was eighteen years old, I went to a service at a rather large church, just as a visitor. I had spoken to this particular pastor a few times, but only casually in passing. That night as he walked up to the pulpit to preach his message he said, "There is a special guest here named Kate, and the Holy Spirit wants her to preach tonight."

I was shocked, because he was not the type of pastor to allow someone to preach from his pulpit unless he knew their ministry very well. I looked around to see if there was another person in the church named Kate. But the pastor pointed to me and said, "There she is. Come on up here, Kate, and minister the Word of God." The Holy Spirit moved powerfully in that service as I watched God's divine favor in operation.

Favor With Church Members

Pastors can eliminate many problems in their churches by claiming favor with the people in their congregations.

Now, do not misunderstand me. I'm not saying this is the solution to every problem in a church! However, because you do have favor, your confession of faith should be that your congregation members are soulwinners, tithers and blessings to your community.

I know a pastor who began to confess that his people were committed and excited about the work of the Lord. One day a guest minister at his church felt led to pray for people who worked in the nursery, children's church, cleaning and in other areas. To the guest minister's surprise, eighty percent of that congregation stood to receive prayer as active workers! The guest minister had never seen such commitment.

That pastor has great favor with the people in his church because he believes for and confesses favor over his congregation daily. By putting the Word to work in your life and ministry, you too can enjoy favor with your church members!

Favor for Souls

The Bible tells us in Second Corinthians 5:18, 19 that we, as believers, have all been entrusted with "the ministry of reconciliation." This means that God has given each of us the privilege and responsibility of telling others the Good News that Jesus saves.

Psalm 2:8 declares that God will give us lost souls for our inheritance when we ask Him. We all need to begin to exercise our faith for winning the lost. We can have favor with people who don't know Jesus. And because we have favor with lost people, they will get saved in our meetings.

Before I go to minister I thank the Lord that I have so much favor with the lost that they come to hear my message. They will receive the message of salvation and be saved. We *do* have favor with the lost, and the angels, who are **ministering spirits, sent forth to minister for them who shall be heirs of salvation** (Hebrews 1:14), will help us as we minister to people with the invitation to receive salvation.

In the book of Acts God reveals His will as thousands of souls were added to the church daily. They gathered from long distances and from the surrounding areas as the Good News of salvation was preached. You, too, can preach the Word with such favor.

So begin to pray and believe God for souls to be added to your account. God desires to work through you to bring many souls into His Kingdom. (Acts 2:47.) Thank the Lord that He is adding to the Church daily such as should be saved!

4
Favor for Finances

4

Favor for Finances

**Beloved, I wish above all things that thou mayest
prosper and be in health, even as thy soul prospereth.**
3 John 2

It is God's will for us to prosper financially, and He has
made provision for us to do it!

Galatians 3:13 declares that we have been redeemed
from the curse of the law. To find out what the curse of the
law is, we must go back to the first five books of the Old
Testament, called the Pentateuch. In reading these books
you will find that the curse of the law included poverty,
sickness and spiritual death.

God promised under the Old Covenant to keep the
people free from poverty and sickness if they kept His
commandments. (Exodus 23:25,26.) God promised them
these things before Jesus ever came. Jesus had not even
died on the cross yet when these people were walking in
God's blessings.

If God promised prosperity under the Old Covenant,
think how much more we, as His children, can partake of
all His goodness under the New and better Covenant!
(Hebrews 8:6.)

One way that you can prosper in finances is through
God's favor. The apostle Peter said in Second Peter 1:2
(AMP):

> **May grace (God's favor) and peace (which is perfect
> well-being, all necessary good, all spiritual prosperity,**

31

and freedom from fears and agitating passions and moral conflicts) be multiplied to you in [the full, personal, precise, and correct] knowledge of God and of Jesus our Lord.

Favor on the Job

You, as a believer, should not be moved according to the world's ways. Your boss may say that they don't give raises where you work. This does not have to apply to you because, as a Christian, you have favor with God and man!

I began expecting and experiencing God's favor in my finances when I was just a teenager. At that time I desperately needed a job that paid well, but some people told me I would never find one because no one would hire a person who had spent most of her life in classes for slow learners.

Despite these negative reports, God was speaking to my heart and assuring me that His desire was for His children to have the very best. Immediately, I began to believe for favor to receive a good job with a good salary.

One day a friend told me about a large company that was hiring. The only catch was that they wanted experienced people, and never in their history had they hired anyone as young as I was.

On my way to the interview, I thanked God that I would have favor with every person in that place. At the interview they asked if I had any experience in the areas for which they were hiring. I told them I could learn fast and that I was the best person for the job. I assured them they would never find anyone as hard-working as me, despite my lack of experience.

Well, against their ordinary procedure, they hired me! It was a wonderful job, with excellent benefits and a good pay scale. I found out that as believers we can have favor on the job!

Favor for Promotion

A good friend shared this story with me a few years ago, and it really blessed my heart. He was a Christian man who began to learn about the favor of God. He started to claim favor on his job. In prayer he asked for favor with his boss and everyone else he worked with, believing that God's divine favor was surrounding him as a shield.

One day his boss called him into his office and said, "We have never done this before, and this doesn't even make sense, but we're giving you a raise." As a result of that raise, this man ended up making more money than his boss did! The employer even told him, "You are the first person in the history of this company who has ever made more money than I have."

Psalm 75:6,7 reminds us that promotion does not come from the east, or west, or south, but from God. We can rely on the favor of God to help us find good jobs and get raises and promotions!

When you are doing your best and meeting, or exceeding, the company's production standards, your boss will be pleased with you and approving of your work. You will be appreciated as a valuable employee. You may feel as though you are giving your all at your job or at your work in the church, but no one is noticing. I want to encourage you to trust God!

Begin to believe God's Word and what He says about His divine favor being bestowed upon you. Know that *God* has already set His affection upon you; He is pleased with you and will cause you to enjoy favor with the people in your workplace as well!

God's Favor Causes Rules to Change

I fly all over the United States to preach. There have been times when an emergency has arisen or revival has broken out in the church where I've been ministering, and I needed to stay longer.

Airline rules don't usually allow tickets to be changed, especially on short notice. One time in particular I called the airline and was told that my ticket could not be changed so that I could fly out several days later.

I prayed and asked God for favor. When I went to the airport to see about it, the person behind the counter said, "We're not really supposed to do this, but we will change the ticket for you today!"

My Aunt May has a great testimony of God's favor working on her behalf. As a widow, she gets most of her income from Social Security. Several years ago she learned that the age for receiving Social Security benefits had been changed because of changes in government policy. That meant she would not receive any more checks until she was older. She desperately needed that money and didn't know how she would support herself without it.

We prayed and agreed for favor. One day, seemingly out of the blue, the Social Security office called to say she would be receiving her checks again!

Not only was this call made on a Saturday (normally government employees don't work on Saturdays!), but she was told, "Your Social Security benefits have been restored." God's favor even works on your behalf with the government!

Joseph Finds Favor in the Sight of God and Man

But the Lord was with Joseph and showed him mercy, and He gave him favor in the sight of the keeper of the prison. And the keeper of the prison committed to Joseph's hand all the prisoners who were in the prison; whatever they did there, it was his doing. The

keeper of the prison did not look into anything that was under Joseph's authority, because the Lord was with him; and whatever he did, the Lord made it prosper.

Genesis 39:21-23 NKJV

Joseph had done nothing wrong when he was thrown into this prison. The wife of his master, Potiphar, had tried to seduce him. When Joseph said no to the desires of the flesh, Potiphar's wife became very angry because he would not give in to her advances.

She decided to get even with Joseph by lying and falsely accusing him of attacking her. As a result, Joseph was thrown into prison. It was unfair. Have you ever been accused of something unfairly? Even unfair accusations cannot keep God's favor from working for you.

God's favor continued to work on Joseph's behalf. We read in Scripture that even being in prison could not keep him down. Joseph had so much favor that the keeper of the prison put all his administrative work in Joseph's hands. Joseph eventually rose to second in command over all of Egypt and ran the whole kingdom for Pharaoh. Now that's favor!

Take the Limits Off God

As a believer, you need not limit your income source to your job. God has many ways and avenues of giving you favor and increasing your income. In my life and ministry I have experienced supernatural favor in finances even in little areas.

For example, I have gotten great deals on office equipment, airline tickets and even a new dress to preach in. Our heavenly Father cares about these small areas of our lives too!

One day I realized that everywhere I go, I experience God's favor. I would be standing in a long line at a grocery store, and another line would just happen to open up. Driving to the shopping mall, I always seemed to find a front-row parking spot. Or a refund check would come in the mail from my insurance company because my rates had gone down unexpectedly.

We must not limit God as to how He chooses to bless us. We must look to Him as our total Source! If you are a minister, do not limit God to your mailbox or by the size of your church.

Let's take the limits off of God and watch His favor work in *every* area of our lives!

5
Favor in Relationships

5

Favor in Relationships

And Jesus increased in wisdom and stature, and in favour with God and man.

Luke 2:52

We already know from Psalm 5:12 that we have favor with God, but we can also have favor with man. (Because the word, *man*, speaks of all mankind, it includes your boss, family members, teachers, pastors, your spouse and others.)

Before going into full-time ministry, I had problems with a certain woman at my job. She was always moody! One day she would be really nice to me, then the next day she would be really nasty. I never knew if she was going to blow up in my face or be nice to me. I felt as though I had to walk on eggshells when I worked near her. (Do you know anybody like this?)

Moody people are usually unhappy and take their frustrations out on the people around them. Often, they will try to control you with their moodiness.

I tried many different ways to solve the problem with this woman. I tried being kind and sweet, but it seemed that when I did she took even greater advantage of me. Then I decided I would be firm and not let her run over me, but that only made matters worse.

One day as I was praying for this woman and the situation, the Lord showed me that I could bind the spirit operating through her and claim favor with her. I needed to take care of this problem in the spirit realm, not in the flesh. (Ephesians 6:12.)

So every day as I went to work, I kept thanking God, standing on the Word and believing Him for favor in this situation.

After about two months, something happened! It seemed as though this woman had been transformed. Every day at work she would go out of her way to bless me and say kind things to me. Her response wasn't phony, either. To this day she is very kind and does things to help me in my ministry!

Favor in Your Marriage

The Word of God says that we can have favor with *all* people. "All people" includes your husband or wife. God desires that married partners grow in favor with one another. But to see God's favor in this area, you cannot be selfish. You must sow favor in order to reap it. (Galatians 6:7.)

Every married person can sow seeds of favor toward his or her spouse by walking in love and preferring the other person before themselves. The Bible instructs us to **walk in love, as Christ also has loved us** (Ephesians 5:2 NKJV) and to **be kindly affectionate to one another with brotherly love, in honor giving preference to one another** (Romans 12:10 NKJV).

Divorce would not be as rampant in the world today if husbands and wives were constantly trying to outdo one another in love.

I know a pastor and his wife who are a great example of God's love. I have been around them a great deal. I can truly say they walk in love toward each other just as much outside the church as they do on Sunday mornings!

They always seem to be trying to outdo one another in love. He loves her as Jesus loves the Church. He treats her as though she is a precious gem. He always opens her car door, helps wash the dishes and brings her a fresh cup of coffee in bed every morning. In return, she is always going out of her way to bake his favorite pie or to cook his favorite meal.

This couple testifies that, at the beginning of their marriage, they promised to love one another and to work through their problems together. They made a rule that the word "divorce" was never to be used in their relationship. After more than twenty-five years, they are still experiencing a happy and successful marriage based upon God's love.

You, too, can have a successful marriage and see God's favor at work. But remember — you must sow favor in order to reap it!

6
Forgiveness Brings Favor

6
Forgiveness Brings Favor

And whenever you stand praying, if you have anything against anyone, forgive him and *let it drop* *(leave it, let it go)*, in order that your Father Who is in heaven may also forgive you your [own] failings and shortcomings and let them drop. But if you do not forgive, neither will your Father in heaven forgive your failings and shortcomings.

Mark 11:25, 26 AMP

If we want to see God's favor in operation, we must walk in forgiveness. We can choose to hold grudges or choose to walk in love and forgiveness.

Forgiveness is not based on how we feel. Instead, we must base our actions on what God's Word says. Just as we believe and pray for things by faith, we can forgive by faith.

When bitter thoughts arise, we must not let our feelings dictate to us. We must walk in love by faith, and our feelings will eventually line up. Jesus is a perfect example of a Man Who walked in forgiveness. By doing so, He brought God's love to the lives of many people.

In Matthew 14 there is a beautiful story of forgiveness. John the Baptist, Jesus' best friend, was brutally murdered — beheaded by King Herod the tetrarch. When Jesus heard the news, He went away to be alone. Most of us, when we hear bad news, do not want to be bothered by people. We just want to be left alone.

Someone found out where Jesus went, and before long a great multitude followed, many of them sick. Instead of attacking Herod, Jesus attacked the devil by healing the sick. The scriptural way to overcome evil is to do good. (Romans 12:21, Matthew 5:44.)

As Jesus walked in love and forgiveness, God showed His favor by pouring out His glory.

Choosing To Forgive

When I first got saved, I was on fire for God. I passed out tracts every day after school and had a burning desire to see people saved. There was just one problem: a girl in my life who had been very mean to me and done me wrong in many ways.

Both the Lord and my mother started dealing with me about forgiving this girl. My mother would hang signs on my bedroom mirror reminding me to pray for her. It wasn't easy at first because my flesh would get in the way when I went to pray. I thought that if I asked God to bless this girl, He just might do it! As you can see, I needed to forgive.

Unfortunately, many of us short-circuit God's power and favor in our lives because we do not realize that unforgiveness hurts *us* more than it hurts the person who wronged us.

Hurting people hurt people. If someone is hurting you, they may very well be hurt and miserable themselves. Romans 5:5 says, **the love of God is shed abroad in our hearts**. We can see from this verse that love for those people already exists in your heart. You *do* love those people. They need your help and prayers.

So putting my feelings aside, I chose to act on God's Word and to pray for my enemies. It was not long before I really felt a love for this person. Soon all the bitterness was gone.

One day when I was home alone, I heard a knock at the front door. The girl who had hated me for so long stood at the entrance. I could not believe my eyes! She told me she just happened to be in the area and wanted to stop by to ask me a question.

She said I had really changed since my salvation experience and wanted to know all about what happened to me. Forgiveness brought God's favor! As I shared the Gospel with her, she was born again and filled with the Holy Spirit right in my own house.

She also told me that because of a problem in her knee, she might have to have an operation. We prayed together about it, and the power of God hit her so hard that she fell to the floor. When she arose, she was totally healed. Glory! Forgiveness brings His favor!

Joseph's Forgiveness Brought Favor

The life of Joseph offers another good example of forgiveness bringing God's favor. Joseph had a great opportunity to walk in bitterness, but instead He chose to pass that opportunity right on by!

Joseph's brothers were jealous of him because their father preferred him. Joseph wore a special coat of many colors that his father made for him. His brothers took the coat from him, killed a goat and put its blood on the garment to convince their father that Joseph was dead.

The brothers sold Joseph to the Ishmaelites for twenty pieces of silver, and those merchants took him to Egypt where he served as a slave.

In Egypt Joseph was lied about and thrown into prison for many years. He went from being the most highly favored member of Jacob's family to living in the lowest dungeon in a foreign land.

Under those circumstances, Joseph had the choice of becoming bitter or better. Without a doubt, he could have become bitter toward his brothers, but instead he chose to please God and become better. Because Joseph forgave those who had done wrong to him, God granted him great favor. He became prison administrator then was freed to become second in command of Egypt.

Forgiveness Releases God's Favor to Others

Joseph's decision to forgive enabled God to bless him abundantly. It also released God's favor for many others. As the second-highest ruler in the land, Joseph was able to bring his entire family out of severe drought into plenty. He saved his ancestry and preserved his family line, from which Jesus was born! I don't know about you, but I'm glad that Joseph chose to forgive his brothers and activate God's favor.

God's Favor Will Work for You

God's favor will work for you as you believe and expect it in your life. These truths from God's Word will change your situation. Expect favor on your job, in your business, your ministry, your family and your social life, and you will never be the same again!

You can walk in favor with God and man!

Twenty Ways
You Can Lose Your Favor

Twenty Ways
You Can Lose Your Favor

In General

1. Don't keep your word.

2. Be rude and pushy.

3. Have a negative attitude.

4. Dress and groom yourself badly.

At Work

5. Always be late/always leave early.

6. Use work time for soulwinning.

7. Complain about your boss.

8. Have a negative attitude.

At Church

9. Don't pay your tithes.

10. Gossip about the pastor.

11. Murmur about how things are done.

12. Don't follow through with commitments.

13. Insist on your own way.

In Relationships

14. Be ungrateful.

15. Take people for granted.

16. Always think of yourself first.

17. Hold a grudge.

At School

18. Don't study or do your homework.

19. Be a smart aleck.

20. Don't obey the rules.

Prayers for Favor

Prayers for Favor

Personal Daily Meditation for Favor

Father, thank You for making me righteous through the blood of Jesus. Because of that, I am blessed and Your favor surrounds me as a shield. When I talk with people, the first thing they come into contact with is my favor shield.

Thank You that I have favor with You and man today. All day long, people go out of their way to bless and help me. I have favor with everyone I deal with today.

I am increasing in wisdom and favor today. I am more than a conqueror in every situation that comes my way.

Because of Your favor upon my life, Lord, I am a delight to people. They enjoy me and take pleasure in being around me. Your willingness and grace make me pleasing and acceptable to everyone I meet today.

Thank You, Father, that You are in me and with me everywhere I go today, so that I am delivered out of every distress and affliction. Everyone I meet sees that I have goodwill and favor and wisdom and understanding, because of your Spirit living in me. In Jesus' name, amen.

Scripture References

Romans 5:9	Luke 2:52
2 Corinthians 5:21	Romans 8:37
Psalm 5:12	Acts 7:9,10 AMP
Proverbs 3:3,4	2 Corinthians 6:16 AMP

Favor in Marriage

Father, I will sow love, patience and kindness toward _____ (name of spouse) today, and as a result, I have favor with them. I am never jealous of them or their time. I am not rude to _____; I always treat them with respect. I don't insist on having my own way, and I'm not touchy or resentful toward _____. I don't keep track of or even pay attention to things they do wrong. I'm happy when things go well, when right and truth prevail. My love for _____ bears up under anything and everything that comes, and I always believe the best of them. My hopes for _____ are fadeless, and my love for _____ never fails.

I purpose to walk in love with _____. I esteem, love, and delight in _____ just as Christ loves me.

Father, thank You that _____ and I are kind and affectionate with each other. I put _____ first and honor _____ before myself, and because of Your favor _____ does the same with me.

Our marriage is flourishing and our prayers are not hindered, because _____ and I walk in love. We are joint heirs of Your unmerited favor, Father. We are united in spirit, and we love each other. We are compassionate, courteous, tenderhearted and humble-minded toward each other. We never return evil for evil or insult for insult. We never scold or berate each other, but we bless each other, praying for each other's welfare, happiness and protection.

_____ and I have favor with You and man; people go out of their way to bless us and our family. In Jesus' name, amen.

Scripture References

Galatians 6:7	Romans 12:10
1 Corinthians 13:4-8 AMP	Romans 8:17
Ephesians 5:2 AMP	Proverbs 3:3,4
1 Peter 3:7-9 AMP	

Favor on the Job

Father, I thank You that promotion doesn't come from the east or the west or the south but from You. Because of Your favor upon me, I will be lifted up and promoted at my job.

Just as You were with Joseph, Lord, so You are with me on my job. Thank You for showing me mercy and lovingkindness and for giving me favor with everyone I come in contact with today, especially my superiors. Thank You for making whatever I do prosper!

Father, I purpose in my heart to be diligent. I am giving my all at what I do for a living, and people are noticing! The world may think that education, brilliance or being well-connected "maketh rich," but even though those things can be helpful, I thank You that Your Word says, **the hand of the *diligent* maketh rich.** Because of You, my superiors like me and favor me. In Jesus' name, amen.

Scripture References

Psalm 75:6,7   Proverbs 10:4

Genesis 39:21-23 AMP

Favor at School

Father, I thank You that I have supernatural favor with my teachers and classmates. I ask You for wisdom, and I believe I am growing in it. Thank You that I have the mind of Christ.

The mighty Holy Spirit lives on the inside of me and helps me to learn quickly. His life and knowledge are in me today.

I can do all things through Christ Who strengthens me. Because of Your favor, Lord, if there's an award to win, I can win it. If there's a scholarship available, it is for me. I am more than a conqueror, in You, Lord. In Jesus' name, amen.

Scripture References

Psalm 5:121

John 4:4 AMP

Luke 2:52

Philippians 4:13

1 Corinthians 2:16

Romans 8:37

Favor in Ministry/Winning the Lost

Father, I thank You for divine favor that supernaturally opens doors of opportunity for me to preach the Gospel, to proclaim the mystery concerning Christ the Messiah. Your favor is working on my behalf, and I do not have to strive in the flesh to get doors to open.

Jesus Christ has reconciled me to You, Father, and given me the ministry of reconciliation. I have favor when I talk to people about You, Lord; they listen to everything I say and are eager to receive You as their Savior.

Father, I ask You to give me the lost people of this world for my inheritance. Thank You that I have favor when I go preach to them.

You are working through me to bring many souls into Your kingdom. You, Father, give me favor and goodwill with all people so that I can preach the Good News of Jesus to them and they can be added to Your kingdom. In Jesus' name, amen.

Scripture References

Colossians 4:3 AMP   Psalm 2:8

2 Corinthians 5:18,19   Acts 2:47 AMP

Favor in Relationships

Father, I thank You for blessing me with good, healthy relationships. I ask You to send me the kind of friends You want me to have. I thank You that Your favor is attracting godly relationships — relationships that will help challenge me spiritually and draw me into a deeper walk with You. Supernaturally remove me from any relationship that would be harmful or would not glorify You.

I ask You, Lord, to give me wisdom in relationships. Help me to be a good friend, one who is led and guided by Your Spirit.

I pray for all of my family relationships. I bind strife and division between me and any family member, and I loose peace and harmony between us. I declare that the enemy is not allowed to cause strife in my family in any way, shape or form. As for me and my house, we will serve You, Lord. I speak that all of my family is saved and we walk in love toward each other. In Jesus' name, amen.

Scripture References

Proverbs 18:24	James 3:16,17
Proverbs 27:17	Matthew 18:18
2 Corinthians 6:14	Joshua 24:15
James 1:5	Acts 16:31

Overcoming Hindrances to Favor

Unforgiveness

I purpose to forgive _____. Because I forgive them, You forgive me, Father, and my prayers are not hindered.

I am bought with a price, the precious blood of Jesus Christ. Therefore, my life is not my own, and I choose Your will over my own, Lord. I'm not directed by my feelings. I cast down thoughts of bitterness and choose to walk in love.

Lord, I ask You to bless _____ in every way today; I pray for their welfare, happiness and protection. I let go of the wrong that _____ has committed against me. I give up any resentment that I feel toward them. I release them and forgive them. I thank You for Your love, forgiveness and favor, Lord. In Jesus' name, amen.

Scripture References

Mark 11:25,26	Luke 6:37 AMP
1 Corinthians 6:20	Luke 11:4
Matthew 6:12-15 AMP	Matthew 5:44
1 Peter 3:9 AMP	

Negative Thinking

I see myself as You see me, Father. I am unconditionally loved and accepted because of the blood Jesus shed for me. I refuse to think thoughts of inferiority and rejection. I have favor with You, Father, and with man, so people treat me well all day long!

I cast down every imagination or picture of myself as insecure, because that is not how You truly see me, Lord. I only think on those things that are obedient and pleasing to You, Lord Jesus — things that are lovely and kind and worthy of praise.

You created and care for me, Father. You have crowned me with glory and honor. Because I am Your child, Your Word says that I have the same glory that You gave to Jesus and that I am one with Him.

I am more than a conqueror through Christ. I am loved completely, totally and unconditionally by the Creator of the universe. You accept me, Father, and I am righteous in Your Son, Jesus Christ. In Jesus' name, amen.

Scripture References

John 3:16	2 Corinthians 10:5
Ephesians 2:4	Psalm 8:4,5
Philippians 4:8 AMP	John 17:22 AMP
Ephesians 1:6	Romans 8:37

Scriptures on Favor

Scriptures on Favor

For thou, LORD, wilt bless the righteous; with favour wilt thou compass him as with a shield.

Psalm 5:12

Let not mercy and truth forsake thee: bind them about thy neck; write them upon the table of thine heart: so shalt thou find favour and good understanding in the sight of God and man.

Proverbs 3:3,4

Glory to God in the highest, and on earth peace to men on whom his favor rests.

Luke 2:14 NIV

For he says, "In the time of my favor I heard you, and in the day of salvation I helped you." I tell you, now is the time of God's favor, now is the day of salvation.

2 Corinthians 6:2 NIV

May the favor of the Lord our God rest upon us; establish the work of our hands for us — yes, establish the work of our hands.

Psalm 90:17 NIV

For the Lord God is a sun and shield; the Lord bestows favor and honor; no good thing does he withhold from those whose walk is blameless.

Psalm 84:11 NIV

Good understanding wins favor, but the way of the unfaithful is hard.

Proverbs 13:15 NIV

He becometh poor that dealeth with a slack hand: but the hand of the diligent maketh rich.

Proverbs 10:4

For whoever finds me [wisdom] finds life and receives favor from the Lord.

Proverbs 8:35 NIV

Obey them [your masters] not only to win their favor when their eye is on you, but like slaves of Christ, doing the will of God from your heart.

Ephesians 6:6 NIV

Slaves, obey your earthly masters in everything; and do it, not only when their eye is on you and to win their favor, but with sincerity of heart and reverence for the Lord.

Colossians 3:22 NIV

For promotion cometh neither from the east, nor from the west, nor from the south. But God is the judge: he putteth down one, and setteth up another.

Psalm 75:6,7

Knowing that whatsoever good thing any man doeth, the same shall he receive of the Lord, whether he be bond or free.

Ephesians 6:8

Bless the Lord, O my soul, and forget not all his benefits:

Who forgiveth all thine iniquities; who healeth all thy diseases;

Who redeemeth thy life from destruction; who crowneth thee with lovingkindess and tender mercies.

Psalm 103:2-4

Nay, in all these things we are more than conquerors through him that loved us.

Romans 8:37

For God so loved the world, that he gave his only begotten Son, that whosoever believeth in him should not perish, but have everlasting life.

John 3:16

But God, who is rich in mercy, for his great love wherewith he loved us.

Ephesians 2:4

To the praise of the glory of his grace, wherein he hath made us accepted in the beloved.

Ephesians 1:6

Much more then, being now justified by his blood, we shall be saved from wrath through him.

Romans 5:9

For he hath made him to be sin for us, who knew no sin; that we might be made the righteousness of God in him.

2 Corinthians 5:21

Ye are of God, little children, and have overcome them: because greater is he that is in you, than he that is in the world.

1 John 4:4

Verily I say unto you, Whatsoever ye shall bind on earth shall be bound in heaven: and whatsoever ye shall loose on earth shall be loosed in heaven.

Again I say unto you, That if two of you shall agree on earth as touching any thing that they shall ask, it shall be done for them of my Father which is in heaven.

Matthew 18:18,19

And when ye stand praying, forgive, if ye have ought against any: that your Father also which is in heaven may forgive you your trespasses.

Mark 11:25

Judge not, and ye shall not be judged: condemn not, and ye shall not be condemned: forgive, and ye shall be forgiven.

Luke 6:37

But I say unto you, Love your enemies, bless them that curse you, do good to them that hate you, and pray for them which despitefully use you, and persecute you.

Matthew 5:44

Not rendering evil for evil, or railing for railing: but contrariwise blessing; knowing that ye are thereunto called, that ye should inherit a blessing.

1 Peter 3:9

Ask of me, and I shall give thee the heathen for thine inheritance, and the uttermost parts of the earth for thy possession.

Psalm 2:8

And they said, Believe on the Lord Jesus Christ, and thou shalt be saved, and thy house.

Acts 16:31

But all things are from God, Who through Jesus Christ reconciled us to Himself [received us into favor, brought us into harmony with Himself] and gave to us the ministry of reconciliation [that by word and deed we might aim to bring others into harmony with Him].

It was God [personally present] in Christ, reconciling and restoring the world to favor with Himself, not counting up and holding against [men] their trespasses [but cancelling them], and committing to us the message of reconciliation (of the restoration to favor).

2 Corinthians 5:18,19 AMP

And Jesus increased in wisdom and stature, and in favour with God and man.

Luke 2:52

Praising God, and having favour with all the people. And the Lord added to the church daily such as should be saved.

Acts 2:47

But the LORD was with Joseph, and shewed him mercy, and gave him favour in the sight of the keeper of the prison.

And the keeper of the prison committed to Joseph's hand all the prisoners that were in the prison; and whatsoever they did there, he was the doer of it.

The keeper of the prison looked not to any thing that was under his hand; because the LORD was with him, and that which he did, the LORD made it to prosper.

Genesis 39:21-23

And the patriarchs, moved with envy, sold Joseph into Egypt: but God was with him,

And delivered him out of all his afflictions, and gave him favour and wisdom in the sight of Pharaoh king of Egypt; and he made him governor over Egypt and all his house.

Acts 7:9,10

An Important Message

If you have never met Jesus Christ, you can know Him today. God cares for you and wants to help you in every area of your life. That is why He sent Jesus to die for you. You can make your life right with God this very moment and make heaven your home.

Pray this prayer now:

Oh, God, I ask You to forgive me of my sins. I believe You sent Jesus to die on the cross for me. I receive Jesus Christ as my personal Lord and Savior. I confess Him as Lord of my life and I give my life to Him. Thank You, Lord, for saving me and for making me new. In Jesus' name, amen.

If you prayed this prayer, I welcome you to the family of God!

Please write to the address that follows and let me know about your decision for Jesus. I want to send you some free literature to help you in your new walk with the Lord.

To contact Kate McVeigh for book, tape,

ministry information, or for prayer, write:

Kate McVeigh Ministries • P. O. Box 690753

Tulsa, Oklahoma 74169-0753

Or call: 1-800-40-FAITH (1-800-403-2484)

Rev. Kate McVeigh travels extensively throughout the United States and abroad, preaching the Gospel of Jesus Christ. She is the author of several books and has many cassette teaching tapes in circulation. Kate's daily radio broadcast, "The Voice of Faith," airs throughout the United States.

Kate is known as a solid minister of the Gospel, with emphasis on healing and winning the lost. Many people have been saved, healed and encouraged in her meetings.

Additional copies of this book

are available from your local bookstore.

Harrison House

Tulsa, Oklahoma 74153

In Canada books are available from:

Word Alive • P. O. Box 670

Niverville, Manitoba • CANADA R0A 1E0

The Harrison House Vision

Proclaiming the truth and the power
Of the Gospel of Jesus Christ
With excellence;

Challenging Christians to
Live victoriously,
Grow spiritually,
Know God intimately.